Incidents, too, must be numerous, however unconnected, to please a London audience: they seem, of late, to expect a certain number, whether good or bad. Quality they are judges of—but quantity they must have.

Still, perhaps, there wants but the pen of genius to give to a play of simple construction, all those attractive powers—which every complex drama is sure to possess.

The following remarkable observation extracted from a critique, on "To Marry, or not to Marry," in a popular Review, is worthy of insertion.

"It is singular that the authoress should, without any foresight, have dramatised the situation of Lord Melville and Mr. Whitbread; yet this she has done: or, at least, circumstances which directly bear on the political relation in which the latter gentleman stands with the former."

DRAMATIS PERSONÆ

Lord Danberry	Mr. Munden
Sir Oswin Mortland	Mr. Kemble
Mr. Willowear	Mr. Farley
Mr. Lavensforth	Mr. Cooke
Amos	Mr. Brunton
Sir Oswin's Servants	Mr. Field
	Mr. Jeffries
	Mr. L. Bologna
	Mr. Lewiss
Lord Danberry's Servant	Mr. Ratchford

Lady Susan Courtly	Mrs. Glover
Mrs. Sarah Mortland	Mrs. Davenport
Hester	Miss Shuttleworth

TO MARRY, OR NOT TO MARRY

ACT THE FIRST

SCENE I

A Hall at the Country Seat of Sir Oswin Mortland.

A loud Knocking at the Gate.

Enter **MRS SARAH MORTLAND**, *followed by a* **SERVANT**.

MRS MORTLAND

Tell the coachman I shan't want the carriage this morning.—And observe, if my brother should ask for me, I am gone to take a walk in the beech grove.

SERVANT
Yes, ma'am.

[Exit **SERVANT**.

[Enter another **SERVANT**.

SERVANT
Ma'am, there's a young lady in a post chaise just stopt at the gate, and says she must see you.

MRS MORTLAND
A young lady!—Must see me!—Who is she?—What is her name?

SERVANT
I asked her name, ma'am, but she refused to tell it.

MRS MORTLAND
Refused to send me her name!—Then pray inform her that I am not at home—tell her I'm busy—I will be seen by no one.

SERVANT
I told her, ma'am, that you were busy, and that you had company, and that you were not at-home; but she says she has come post more than twenty miles on purpose to pay you a visit, and cannot return without seeing you.

MRS MORTLAND
What an impertinent!—Come post!—show her in—how extremely ridiculous and ill bred!

SERVANT
Here she is, ma'am.

[Exit **SERVANT**.

[Enter **HESTER**, in great agitation.

MRS MORTLAND
My dear Miss —! It is Miss —, the young lady I met at Beverley—is it not?—What in the name of wonder—

HESTER
Oh, Mrs. Sarah Mortland!—Oh, madam, pity and forgive me!—forgive this intrusion, and pity the cause of it.

MRS MORTLAND [Dissatisfiedly]
My dear, I must forgive all you do.

To Marry Or Not To Marry by Mrs Inchbald

A COMEDY, IN FIVE ACTS

AS PERFORMED AT THE THEATRE ROYAL COVENT GARDEN

Elizabeth Simpson was born on 15th October 1753 at Stanningfield, near Bury St Edmunds, Suffolk.

Despite the fact that she suffered from a debilitating stammer she was determined to become an actress.

In April 1772, Elizabeth left, without permission, for London to pursue her chosen career. Although she was successful in obtaining parts her audiences, at first, found it difficult to admire her talents given her speech impediment. However, Elizabeth was diligent and hard-working on attempting to overcome this hurdle. She spent much time concentrating on pronunciation in order to eliminate the stammer. Her acting, although at times stilted, especially in monologues, gained praise for her approach for her well-developed characters.

That same year she married Joseph Inchbald and a few months later they appeared for the first time together on stage in 'King Lear'. The following month they toured Scotland with the West Digges's theatre company. This was to continue for several years.

Completely unexpectedly Joseph died in June 1779. It was now in the years after her husband's death that Elizabeth decided on a new literary path. With no attachments and acting taking up only some of her time she decided to write plays.

Her first play to be performed was 'A Mogul Tale or, The Descent of the Balloon', in 1784, in which she also played the leading female role of Selina. The play was premiered at the Haymarket Theatre.

One of the things that separated Elizabeth from other contemporary playwrights was her ability to translate plays from German and French into English for an audience that was ever-hungry for new works.

Her success as a playwright enabled Elizabeth to support herself and have no need of a husband to support her. Between 1784 and 1805 she had 19 of her comedies, sentimental dramas, and farces (many of them translations from the French) performed at London theatres. She is usually credited as Mrs Inchbald.

Mrs Elizabeth Inchbald died on 1st August 1821 in Kensington, London.

Index of Contents
REMARKS
DRAMATIS PERSONÆ
TO MARRY, OR NOT TO MARRY
ACT THE FIRST

SCENE I - A Hall at the Country Seat of Sir Oswin Mortland
SCENE II - A Library
ACT THE SECOND
SCENE I - The Library
SCENE II - A Parlour
ACT THE THIRD
SCENE I - A Forest, and a Ruined Cottage
SCENE II - A Saloon at Lord Danberry's, with Folding Doors into a Garden
ACT THE FOURTH
SCENE I - An Apartment at Sir Oswin Mortland's
ACT THE FIFTH
SCENE I - The Forest and Cottage
SCENE II - An Apartment at Sir Oswin's
MRS INCHBALD – A SHORT BIOGRAPHY
MRS INCHBALD – A CONCISE BIBLIOGRAPHY

REMARKS

It appears as if the writer of this play had said, previous to the commencement of the task, "I will shun the faults imputed by the critics to modern dramatists; I will avoid farcical incidents, broad jests, the introduction of broken English, whether Hibernian or provincial; songs, processions, and whatever may be considered by my judges as a repetition of those faults of which they have so frequently complained."

Vain is the forecast of both man and woman!—Supposing all those evils escaped which the authoress dreaded, what is the event of her cautious plan?—Has she produced a good comedy?—No. She has passed from one extreme to another; and, attempting to soar above others, has fallen even beneath herself.

In the dearth of wit, an audience will gladly accept of humour: but the author who shall dare to exclude from his comedy the last, without being able to furnish the first, assuredly must incur the rigorous, though just sentence, of dulness.

There is a degree of interest in the fable of "To Marry, or not to Marry," which protected it on the stage, and may recommend it to the reader. The characters of Sir Oswin, Mrs. Sarah Mortland, Hester, and her father, are all justly drawn, but not with sufficient force for high dramatic effect. Their serious tendency wants relief from characters of more risible import, or from more comic materials contained in themselves. They are elegant and natural, but not powerful in any of their diversified attempts upon the heart.

Simplicity, the first design in the composition of this play, is perhaps, for the accomplishment of theatrical success, the most difficult of all attainments.

The stage delights the eye far oftener than the ear. Various personages of the drama, however disunited, amuse the looker on; whilst one little compact family presents a sameness to the view, like unity of place; and wearies the sight of a British auditor fully as much.

HESTER
I thought so, madam—I hoped you would forgive me, when I resolved to take this liberty. The kindness, the partiality you showed towards me, the very first time I was in your company—

MRS MORTLAND
And which was the last, I believe, my dear; for I think I never saw you but once in my life.

HESTER
No, madam; at Mrs. Brian's ball, when you were there at Beverley races. But that once you praised my dancing, my singing, my conversation!—You said, if you remember, that you wished you had just such a young companion as I was; you told me you should be glad to see me at any time—and so I am come.

MRS MORTLAND [Disconcerted]
Well!—and I am glad, very glad to see you.—I don't say I'm not.—Only a little surprised, my dear, that you did not wait for a more formal invitation.

HESTER
What it wanted in form, you made up with earnestness.

MRS MORTLAND
And I then, at that time, felt all the ardour I expressed. But, my dear, are you come by yourself?

HESTER
Did you wish me to bring any body else?

MRS MORTLAND [Hastily]
No, no.

HESTER [Weeps]
I thought you would not—so I flew to you all alone, in my distress.

MRS MORTLAND
But what distress? And why are you in tears?—I hope you have not run away from your friends?

HESTER
I have no friend but you.

MRS MORTLAND
Hem! hem!
[Confounded]
But, my dear, tell me what is all this about? And why—
[Frightened, and angry]
—have I the pleasure of seeing you here?

HESTER
You know that I am an orphan!

MRS MORTLAND
Yes—that I was told—but I really forget your name.

HESTER
My christian name is Hester—and when I am called by any other, it is that of my guardian, with whom I have lived from my infancy—Mr. Ashdale.

MRS MORTLAND
Hester Ashdale.

HESTER
For my guardian never speaks of my own family but with reproach; has seldom permitted me to ask him any questions concerning them; and, indeed, has ever treated me with cruelty!

[Weeping.

MRS MORTLAND
We all have our trials, and we ought all to submit to them.

HESTER
But mayn't we run away from them?

MRS MORTLAND
Not always. Pray, when did you leave your guardian's house?

HESTER
This very morning.—This very morning I was to have been married—and they are now all waiting for me at the church, or by this time gone home to a very uncomfortable dinner without me.

MRS MORTLAND
Without the bride!—Was there ever—

HESTER
But, if you knew the intended bridegroom, you would not wonder.—He is so odious to me, that I had rather stay with you by half, and be your companion or servant.—I'll read—I'll sing—I'll work—I'll do every thing to please you.

MRS MORTLAND
But, my dear, this house I cannot call my own.—It is, in fact, my brother's, Sir Oswin Mortland's.—As I live entirely in the country, he suffers me to pass for the mistress of it, but at present, he's down here himself; and though much younger than I am, yet he is so much richer and wiser than I am, that he commands me in every thing. Indeed, such is his temper, he will always be lord and master of every place into which he condescends to enter; and he hates intruders—strangers—strange ladies in particular.

HESTER
Then why did you invite me to come?

MRS MORTLAND
I invited you—but I did not fix the time.

HESTER
No, madam—but I thought I might.

MRS MORTLAND
Then, your indiscretion in quitting your guardian's house, and your intended, husband!—Why did you give your consent to marry?

HESTER
I was in such fear of my guardian's anger, and his wife's peevishness—I had no sense, no skill, no argument to answer all they said to prevail on me! It was, beside, so ill bred to tell a gentleman that I could not love him—that I could not bear to live with him—that he was disagreeable to me!

MRS MORTLAND
So, then, you consented without any apparent reluctance!

HESTER
I am sure I looked reluctantly: but I was obliged to say yes, to all they asked of me.

MRS MORTLAND
Then you should have kept your word.

HESTER
Indeed and so I intended, till it came to the very last—then I planned my escape. Did you never resolve on a thing, and think you would do it whatever it cost you: then, just on the point when it was to be done, find your heart sink, and all your resolutions turn to nothing?

MRS MORTLAND
It must have been some very shocking husband they designed for you, to give you such an aversion!

HESTER
Oh, he was not so very bad neither!—I dare say you would have had no objection to marry him: but I always said to myself—"I think a wedding is so pleasant;—the bells ring so sweetly; the bride and the bridesmaids look so nice; and every one so joyful—that I never will marry, unless I can be joyful too."

MRS MORTLAND
But when you return to your guardians, what do you think they will say to you for this conduct?

HESTER
I never mean to return, madam; and by the time I have lived a week or two here, perhaps you may never wish me to go back.

MRS MORTLAND
"A week or two!"—"never go back!"—I must instantly acquaint Sir Oswin with this visit, and obtain his permission, before I can venture to say you shall stay here even an hour or two.

HESTER
Then dear, dear Mrs. Sarah Mortland, as this Sir Oswin is a cross, illnatured man, don't say I ran away just as I was going to be married: it may make him think me to blame.

MRS MORTLAND
Tell him that!—Not for the universe!—If I were, he would not merely turn you out of his house, but me, for suffering you to come into it.—Step into that room while I go to him.

HESTER
Oh, madam! rash as I may seem in having ventured hither, my heart has beat with fear more than with hope. Pity me as a stranger, if not as an acquaintance, and reflect that on my reception here, depends all my future prospects.

[Exit **HESTER**

MRS MORTLAND
I vow she has put me in such a fright!—What can I say to Sir Oswin? I did ask her to come and see me, to be sure; and it would be uncharitable to turn her out; and yet it was equally uncharitable to come on such a slight invitation.

[Exit.

SCENE II

A Library.

SIR OSWIN MORTLAND discovered reading.

LORD DANBERRY raps at the Door twice.

SIR OSWIN
Who's there?

[Enter **LORD DANBERRY**.

LORD DANBERRY
Nephew! nephew!—I beg your pardon; I know you don't like to be interrupted in your studies.

SIR OSWIN
Yet my friends generally break in upon me at those very times, my lord, and tell me.—"they know they are disobliging me,"—by way of apology.

LORD DANBERRY
Well, but you will excuse me—you'll excuse me, I fear, sooner than my errand; for that, I know you'll be displeased with.

SIR OSWIN
Another apology!

LORD DANBERRY
Nephew, it does not signify, but I must ask you, again and again,—will you suffer my fine estate, and our old title, to go to a mere stranger? This, you know, must be the case, if you resolve to continue a bachelor.—The thought of it embitters my life. Consider, Sir Oswin, marriage, as I have often told you, is a duty every man in your situation owes to his family, to society, to—

SIR OSWIN [With vehemence]
Well, well, I grant it, my dear uncle; and as my temper cannot bear continual irritation, I shall comply with your request, to get rid of it for ever.—I will marry, to put an end to all your anxieties, though I had rather—

LORD DANBERRY
Thank you, my dear nephew, for this hearty promise: you have made me happy.

SIR OSWIN
And myself miserable. I never thought of becoming a husband. I never intended to be a husband. Marriage will interfere with my pursuits, my studies, my—

LORD DANBERRY [Soothingly]
You will like the marriage state better than you expect.

SIR OSWIN
Why, my lord, I shall at least meet with no disappointments in it. For I do, with certainty, expect that it will progressively destroy every comfort of my life; and I shall fortify myself against their total extinction.

LORD DANBERRY
I own the prospect for a married man is not very bright just at this precise period. But, without dwelling on your character as a husband, consider the happiness you may enjoy as a parent. Reflect upon a son and heir!

SIR OSWIN
I can feel no happiness in contemplating what does not exist.

LORD DANBERRY
But I can. I can experience the highest gratification in foreseeing that now a son of yours will inherit my title and estates when I am laid low: for, by the course of years, I have but a short time to live.

SIR OSWIN
So my marriage, which will inevitably rob me of every enjoyment I possess, is to accommodate two nonentities; one of whom will be gone out of the world, and the other not come into it!

LORD DANBERRY
Still, there is a being in full existence, in the bloom of life, to whom your marriage will give high delight. The lady, with whom I mean you to marry—Lady Susan Courtly.

SIR OSWIN
Lady Susan Courtly!

LORD DANBERRY
Yes;—and who, I believe, is as much in love with you—

[**SIR OSWIN** goes to him, and looks him stedfastly in the Face.

SIR OSWIN
My lord—I am between thirty and forty years of age. I have lived in the world, at least half those years, an observer.

LORD DANBERRY
I know you have.

SIR OSWIN
And do you talk to me of being in love?

LORD DANBERRY
Not you, but the lady. The lady, I say, is in love. Lady Susan.

[**SIR OSWIN** turns away.

SIR OSWIN
Psha! psha! psha!

LORD DANBERRY
She fancies she is.

SIR OSWIN
But she won't make me fancy she is.

LORD DANBERRY
I know you don't believe there is such a thing, as what is usually meant by the word love. But don't you think there may be such a thing as a good wife?

SIR OSWIN [After Consideration]
Yes, 'faith, I think there may. I think, possibly, there may.

LORD DANBERRY
And why shou'dn't such a one fall to your share?

SIR OSWIN
O, my lord,—It would be unconscionable in me to expect it. I can't hope to monopolize rarity.

LORD DANBERRY
Ay, you are jocose; you may make free with your old uncle.

[SIR OSWIN takes his Hand kindly, as if apologizing.

And now I'll tell you how your old uncle has made free with you. I have brought down Lady Susan Courtly to my house, here in the country—on this very spot—in the firm persuasion that you are smitten with her charms: but that you are too grave, too reserved, too consequential, think too much of your own importance and perfections, to ask a favour, even of a lady.

SIR OSWIN
Why, my lord!—

LORD DANBERRY
So, to save your dignity from the humiliation of sighing and kneeling, I have, in your name, solicited her hand in marriage.

SIR OSWIN
My lord, I should be very sorry you appeared ridiculous in this affair.

LORD DANBERRY
I knew you would—you always were careful of my reputation, and therefore I knew you would acknowledge, as yours, every syllable I have said in your name.

SIR OSWIN [Walking about in agitation]
Here's the beginning of matrimony! Always false foundations!

LORD DANBERRY
But tell me: Don't you like Lady Susan, now, as well as you like any other woman?

SIR OSWIN
Quite as well—she is the same to me as her whole sex. I have no partiality to any one, nor dislike to any one, except as a wife.

LORD DANBERRY
Human foresight is truly exemplified in me! My pride has been to make you a learned man, a man of erudition. And what is my reward? You love nothing but books.

SIR OSWIN
Yes, my lord, I love the whole human race—and I love my books, because they have taught me to do so.

LORD DANBERRY
Can you boldly repeat that you love all mankind? There is one man whom I am sure you exclude from the rest.

SIR OSWIN
You mean the state delinquent, Lavensforth—a man who has attempted my life?

LORD DANBERRY
Not directly.

SIR OSWIN
Pardon me, my lord;—his challenge was a direct attempt: and though the laws interfered, and disappointed that hope of his revenge; yet I have reason to believe he did not give up his designs against me, even when he left the kingdom.

LORD DANBERRY
That is now full thirteen years ago; and if he be still living—

SIR OSWIN
He is rancorous still: his rage was of no transient nature.—Yes, I own I do not love the man, who can bear malice for an act of justice; or could impute to my clear motives in his impeachment, any other end than the public good.

LORD DANBERRY
But the public took such interest in the cause,—Your triumph was so popular, and his defeat so—

SIR OSWIN
Ay, that defeat, as well as his consequent punishment, may have been too severe; for though his sentence reached only to a fine, yet ultimately it proved so heavy, that, in effect, it caused his exile.

LORD DANBERRY
So much the better.

SIR OSWIN
And, after all—though one may be ruined, and another raised to fame, by rigorous prosecution of the faults of office; yet, in the candid estimate of man's imperfections and man's virtues, the accuser is seldom entirely right, nor the accused totally wrong.

LORD DANBERRY
Why, I never heard you talk thus before—nor would I have the world hear you now. You did not speak thus on Lavensforth's impeachment.

SIR OSWIN
No!—Youthful ardour made me then pronounce with decision. Years of studious application, and more matured experience, have lessened my confidence in my own opinions.

LORD DANBERRY
Ay, you are in an ill humour now, and so you'll contradict every thing I assert. I am glad, however, to hear you speak so diffidently of your own judgment, for then you can the better rely on mine, and keep the promise you have made me.

SIR OSWIN
Yes—my lord—as I have said, I'll marry in obedience to your will—I'll keep my word.

LORD DANBERRY [Taking hold of him kindly]
But now when? When will you fix the happy day? When will you marry?

[**SIR OSWIN** considers.

Why, as you have no great inclination for the business, don't delay—marry soon—as you don't like it, get it over at once.

SIR OSWIN
"Get it over?" Why, it's to last for life.

LORD DANBERRY
Not always. There is such a thing as benefit of survivorship.

[MRS SARAH MORTLAND raps at the Library Door.

SIR OSWIN
Come in.

LORD DANBERRY
Then I'll go. And I'll go out at this door, that I mayn't meet your company.

[Going, returns.

And much obliged to you, my dear nephew, I am for all you have promised—I'm sure Lady Susan will be—

[Rapping again at the Library Door.

SIR OSWIN
Come in.

[Calling very loud.

[Exit LORD DANBERRY.

[Enter MRS SARAH MORTLAND.

MRS MORTLAND
To tell you the truth, I am half afraid to come in.

SIR OSWIN
Because I have told you a thousand times, you may command any part of my day but this.

[Enter LORD DANBERRY.

LORD DANBERRY
I beg pardon,—I'll tell her you'll call on her to-day, or to-morrow morning.

[Exit.

SIR OSWIN [Impatiently]

My lord!—You need not be afraid, however, sister; for, at present, your intrusion is not unwelcome.

[Sits down.

MRS MORTLAND
Nay, I am not so much alarmed at my intrusion, as at my errand: for I am come to tell you something you won't like.

SIR OSWIN
More things I don't like, and more apologies! Why, then—
[Very cross]
—you have chosen a bad time for your bad news, for I am in a very ill temper.

MRS MORTLAND
The reason I came now was—that you might not be more offended at dinner time, by meeting a stranger at table. It is hard I can't make you love strangers!

SIR OSWIN
Why won't you be content with my loving you?—Why won't you be contented with my loving all my old, troublesome, tiresome friends? If I loved the company of every idle stranger, ten to one I could not endure yours.

MRS MORTLAND
That I would pardon, could I once see you enjoy society like other people. But, I believe, I shall soon begin to think you have taken two of the monastic vows; that of seclusion, and the other against marriage.

SIR OSWIN
In the latter, I shall at least, boast of your example.

MRS MORTLAND
You are mistaken—I never made a vow against marriage. It was the men, I believe, who vowed never to ask me the question. Let me tell you, brother, there is a great deal of difference in sentiment, between a single man of a certain age, and a single woman of a certain age. The one does not marry, because he won't:—the other, because she can't.—But we'll not talk of these things now.—
[Approaching him with Insinuation]
It's only a pretty girl is to dine with us to-day.

SIR OSWIN [Rising, in Anger]
What have I to do with pretty girls?

MRS MORTLAND
I said so,—I thought so;—I knew you would not like of her coming.

SIR OSWIN
Then why did you invite her?

MRS MORTLAND

I only invited her in the usual complimentary way; told her I should be glad to see her at any time; begged she would make this house her home, if she came into this part of the world. She lived twenty miles off, and I never imagined—

SIR OSWIN
Oh, that every ostentatious invitation was just so received!

MRS MORTLAND
I own that I did wrong; and therefore have taken her in for a few days.

SIR OSWIN
"A few days!"—For yourself, you are justly repaid: for me, I will have no annoyance from your visitors. I shall set off for London to-morrow morning.

MRS MORTLAND
Nay, nay—why, she won't be in your way—You will never see her, but at breakfast, dinner, and supper.

SIR OSWIN
So,—she's only to torment me from morning till night.

MRS MORTLAND
—One of the most beautiful young women!

SIR OSWIN
What's her beauty to me?

MRS MORTLAND
An orphan—without parents to protect her—without a single relation, that she knows, on earth—

[He pays Attention.

Has been so cruelly used!—You won't go to town, will you?

SIR OSWIN
I don't know.

MRS MORTLAND
—If you had seen how the poor creature wept when she arrived, and hung on me for pity!—You'll dine with us to-day?

SIR OSWIN [Sitting down]
Perhaps I may.

MRS MORTLAND
—And you'll behave civilly to this poor girl? I'll tell you who she is.

SIR OSWIN
No, no; I don't want to know who she is.

MRS MORTLAND
—Her distress is so great!

SIR OSWIN
Why, then I don't care who she is.

[He begins writing.

[Pause between them.

MRS MORTLAND
Well, brother, now, I suppose, I have your leave to go?

SIR OSWIN
How can you doubt it?

[Exit **MRS MORTLAND**.—The Scene closes on **SIR OSWIN** writing.

ACT THE SECOND

SCENE I

The Library.

SIR OSWIN discovered writing still.

WILLOWEAR [Without]
I tell you, I'm sure he will see me. Tell him, I come on very particular business.

[Enter **SERVANT**.

SERVANT
Mr. Willowear.

SIR OSWIN
Mr. Willowear, my old acquaintance and school-fellow!—Show him in.

[Exit **SERVANT**.

I thought he was too fond of London, ever to come such a distance from it.

[Rises.

What can be his particular business with me?

[Enter **WILLOWEAR**.

WILLOWEAR
Sir Oswin, I have taken this liberty—

SIR OSWIN
Mr. Willowear, you tremble!—What causes this agitation?

WILLOWEAR
The cause is, I am in a passion—and I can hardly tell my story for anger.

SIR OSWIN
You are not angry with me, I hope?

WILLOWEAR
No; Heaven forbid—But you will excuse me, if I say, I am offended with some part of your family.

SIR OSWIN
Show me in what any of them have used you ill, and you shall have instant redress. Pray sit down.

[They sit.

WILLOWEAR
I am sorry to name a lady of your family—a lady, whom I have not the honour of knowing—your sister.

SIR OSWIN
My sister!

WILLOWEAR
Yes; and another lady has used me worse, and has flown to her for protection.

SIR OSWIN
I have just been quarrelling with my sister, for taking a young woman into the house. Does she belong to you?

WILLOWEAR
She was within.—To tell you the whole story, Sir Oswin: the other day I fell in love.

SIR OSWIN
Ha! ha! ha!

WILLOWEAR
A beautiful girl!—You might have done the same thing.

SIR OSWIN
No, no;—Ha! ha! ha! I beg your pardon. Proceed with your story—Ha! ha! ha! you know I was never in love.

WILLOWEAR
But can you pretend to say, you never shall!

SIR OSWIN [Looking stedfastly at him]
Yes, I can.—But proceed.

WILLOWEAR
A little, friendless girl! hardly any body knew who! brought up by the apothecary of our village. She caught my eye—her simple manners won my heart. I admire simplicity, of all female qualities.

SIR OSWIN
So do I.

WILLOWEAR
I grew tired of leading a bachelor's life. I had seen you, Sir Oswin, for instance, often out of temper—crabbed and rugged. No other fault, you know, ever laid to your charge, than being a little sullen, morose, and rather imperious. But all this, the women said, was merely for want of a wife.

SIR OSWIN
"The women said!"—My dear sir, pray go on with your story. Does this young lady, in my house, belong to you?

WILLOWEAR
Yes—no—she was very near it, though—I won't say how very, very near it; for then you'll laugh again, and with some reason.

SIR OSWIN
What! I suppose the ring bought.

WILLOWEAR
The book opened—when she took it in her head to run away.

SIR OSWIN [Rises]
Monstrous! abominable! not to be borne! She has imposed on my sister with some piteous tale.—But she sha'n't remain here a moment longer.

WILLOWEAR
I thought you would not suffer it.

SIR OSWIN
Certainly not.

[Rings the Bell.

WILLOWEAR
How she contrived to have every thing ready to make her escape, no one can guess. But, instead of meeting me in the church, where I was waiting with a few friends, impatient for her coming, she slipped from her bridemaids into a postchaise, and drove to your house, where I have traced her.

SIR OSWIN
Who's there?

[Enter **SERVANT**.

Tell my sister I desire to see her, and the lady (the young woman who came hither this morning) in the parlour by the saloon immediately.

[Exit **SERVANT**.

Depend upon it, she shall leave this house instantly, or give me the very best reasons why she should not.

WILLOWEAR
She can give you none—after encouraging my addresses, accepting my presents—for I gave her trinkets in abundance, and a diamond ring of great value,—In a word, I myself, am the only gift she ever refused.

SIR OSWIN
And, does she expect a refuge under my roof, thus charged with robbery?

WILLOWEAR
The goods are upon her, I dare say. But, after all, I would rather have her back, than my property. She is more precious to me than my diamond.

SIR OSWIN
"Precious! Have her back!" Wish to have such a woman for a wife!

WILLOWEAR
Very true—I am wrong, I own—but, love! love!—Notwithstanding your sneer, Sir Oswin, love is every thing.

SIR OSWIN
No, 'tis nothing—a whim—a fancy, conceived by the infirmity of youth, or of age. At seventeen or seventy, the infatuation is excusable; but, at your time of life, and mine, oh! it sinks the man into the boy, or dotard. But, come, I'll show you to my plantations, where you may amuse yourself, while I talk to these women; and, depend on my settling this business with as much care and concern for your welfare, as if I had your faith in the omnipotence of love.

[Exeunt.

SCENE II

A Parlour

Enter **MRS SARAH MORTLAND** and **HESTER**

MRS MORTLAND
Come, come—don't tremble thus—don't cry thus—don't be thus alarmed.

HESTER
Is not Sir Oswin coming to talk to me? perhaps to put himself in a passion—to turn me out of the only place I have to shelter me.

MRS MORTLAND
He has merely sent word, he wishes to speak to us; and will most likely be as angry with me as with you.

HESTER
You are accustomed to his sternness.

MRS MORTLAND
Stern as he is, he has the best of hearts to those who deserve his kindness.

HESTER
But I know myself undeserving.

MRS MORTLAND
And your disappointed lover, who has certainly come to Sir Oswin on your account, has, no doubt, painted your conduct in the very worst colours.

HESTER
Dear madam, let me run away again;—suffer me to go before Sir Oswin comes, and save me the disgrace of being turned out.

MRS MORTLAND
No; I should be turned out myself, if I were to connive at your escape. There is one circumstance, however, relative to you, that I do wish concealed from my brother, because it increases the peril of your situation.

HESTER
Dear madam, what is it?

MRS MORTLAND
Your guardian has sent me a letter by this Mr. Willowear, in which he informs me, that your real name is Lavensforth, and that you are the daughter, the only child, of Sir Oswin's inveterate enemy. By this intelligence, your guardian conceives you will be immediately restored to him, as my brother, under such circumstances, would not suffer you to remain a moment longer here.

HESTER
Yes, madam, I am the child of an unfortunate man, whom I never heard mentioned without reproach. I knew he had many enemies, and for that reason I was denied my right to be called by his name: but I did not know that Sir Oswin was his particular foe.

MRS MORTLAND

Yes; and though, possibly, both of them good men, peculiar occurrences, in the earlier part of their lives, when Sir Oswin was very young indeed, made them the bitterest enemies.

HESTER
Oh, then, my dear, dear madam, do not tell Sir Oswin who I am, till I am gone away—Indeed, I'll go the moment he has seen me.—But, if you please, I had rather go now.

MRS MORTLAND
Do you think Mr. Willowear has told my brother who you are?

HESTER
No; I am sure Mr. Willowear does not know himself: for my guardian, fearing he might object to my father's misfortunes, always charged me to conceal my real name from him.

MRS MORTLAND
Then, I promise you, my brother shall never know it from me. Your guardian, indeed, enjoins me silence to all but Sir Oswin; of course, he can hear it no other way. And this secret of your birth, Mr. Ashdale adds in his letter, was in consequence of a promise your father extorted, when he left you to his care.

HESTER
My father made him promise also, he would treat me with kindness; but in that, he never kept his word.

MRS MORTLAND
You remember your father then?

HESTER
Yes, yes; I shall always remember him; though, I fear, he has forgot me.

MRS MORTLAND
You think, he is still living?

HESTER
I hope so! but, for these two last years, no letter—no—

MRS MORTLAND
Hush! hush! Sir Oswin!

[**HESTER** hangs down her Head.

[Enter **SIR OSWIN**—he passes his Sister, and stands between her and **HESTER**.

SIR OSWIN [After looking sternly at each]
My business with you, madam, and with this young person, will be very shortly concluded.
[To his **SISTER**]
It is merely to express my displeasure, and to express it with warmth such as I feel, that I have been imposed upon by you.
[To **HESTER**]
And that a worthy man has been imposed upon by you.

MRS MORTLAND
Brother, we have both done wrong, and both hope for pardon.

SIR OSWIN
Amendment must precede forgiveness. She must return with her future husband.

HESTER
Ah! Ah!

[Screaming.

SIR OSWIN [Roughly]
What do you mean?

HESTER
Oh, sir! did you know what it was to have a horror of being married!

SIR OSWIN [Shrinks and hesitates]
Well,—well,—suppose I did know, what then?

HESTER
Then, you would pity me.

SIR OSWIN [Aside]
The poor girl has a repugnance to marriage, and I compassionate her.

MRS MORTLAND
For my part, brother, though I have taken this young lady in, yet I have lectured her.

SIR OSWIN
You "lecture her!" And by what authority have you lectured her?

MRS MORTLAND
Ha! you think nobody is to give lectures but yourself.

SIR OSWIN [Going near to **HESTER**]
How old are you?

HESTER
I am near seventeen.

SIR OSWIN
I should not have thought you so much!

HESTER
No; for not being used to fashionable company, I have nothing to say in conversation—except what I think.

SIR OSWIN
'Would to heaven all your sex had no more to utter. The family in which you lived, your guardian, I suppose, used his influence to persuade you to marry?

HESTER
Yes; and Mr. Willowear used his influence to persuade me too; but I had rather not.

SIR OSWIN
I don't blame your being nice, and cautious, in respect to marriage; but you should not have given your lover hopes.

HESTER
I could not tell him to his face, that I hated him.

SIR OSWIN
But, you received his presents.

HESTER
It was the only favour I ever granted, and he asked a thousand.

SIR OSWIN
Favours!

HESTER
He called them so. He said, he did not value the things he gave me, but for their being mine. Here is his great present of all—a diamond ring! Will you have it? I shall give it with as much pleasure to you, as he gave it to me, I dare say—and shall think it a greater favour.

SIR OSWIN [To his Sister]
This is a very singular girl you have introduced to me!

MRS MORTLAND
And I have introduced as singular a man to her—therefore, I trust, you will understand one another.

SIR OSWIN
For my part, she has taken my understanding away.

MRS MORTLAND
And as, I believe, she herself never had any, you will agree better and better.

SIR OSWIN [To **HESTER**]
I shall take this ring, and return it to its first possessor.—And, now, as you intend to abandon him, and your former home, what do you design to do?
[A Pause]
—Whither do you intend to go?

HESTER

I did intend to stay here. But, I suppose, you won't suffer it; though Mrs. Sarah Mortland invited me, or I should not have made so free as to come.

MRS MORTLAND
Upon my word,—I only—

SIR OSWIN
Hush! Hold your tongue.—I want to hear her talk, not you.—And would you be content to stay, and give up all your friends?

HESTER
I hope I should find friends here.

SIR OSWIN
You have no parents? no relations, I am told?

HESTER
My mother died, when I was an infant.—My father went abroad,—perhaps is dead too: I never knew any other relations, and I hardly know my own surname; for I am always called Hester.

SIR OSWIN
—A Mr. and Mrs. Ashdale brought you up?

HESTER
But were so unkind to me, that I durst not tell them I wouldn't marry;—and, I hope, you will not send me back with a man I cannot love.

SIR OSWIN
Then, you never loved him?

HESTER
O! no, no.

SIR OSWIN
Nor ever loved any other man?

HESTER
O, no, never, never.

SIR OSWIN
Nor ever could, I suppose?

HESTER [After looking at him, unconsciously, from Head to Foot]
Yes,—yes,—yes,—O, yes.—I think I could.

SIR OSWIN
I thought you said, you had set your heart against marriage.

HESTER
No I have not.—No, no—but I should like to chuse my own husband.

SIR OSWIN
How chuse? Women can't make love.

HESTER
But they can listen.—And I'll never listen, but where the sound is sweet.

SIR OSWIN [To his **SISTER**]
I don't know how I can turn this girl out of the house. Poor creature!
[Affecting a smile of contempt]
She has lost her mother, and is not sure whether or no she has a father.

MRS MORTLAND
Then, do you be a father to her.

SIR OSWIN
Is there such difference in our ages?—She's seventeen, and I am not above—

MRS MORTLAND
No; but I have been so used to hear you call yourself an old man—

SIR OSWIN
I beg your pardon, if I have—for that's making my elder sister a very old woman.

MRS MORTLAND
Well, and I shall have no objection to being an old woman, while it is a privilege of that state to be of service to the young ones.

HESTER
And you have been of great service to me—thank you—thank you.

SIR OSWIN
Yes, sister—you are a very good woman, I believe; and if I do find fault with you, now and then, it is because I wish you to be my companion, and my companion to be as perfect as possible.—Yes indeed—I think you have done quite right in sheltering this poor orphan—and I recommend her to your further protection.

[Passing **MRS MORTLAND** over to **HESTER**.

MRS MORTLAND [Going, returns]
You'll dine with us, Sir Oswin?

SIR OSWIN [Considering]
Why, yes; I don't know that I am going any where—yes—I'll dine with you.

[Exeunt **MRS MORTLAND** and **HESTER**, the latter courtesying low to **SIR OSWIN**.

Poor girl! I really feel for her—poor girl!

[He walks about, moves the Chairs and Table—at last he takes up a Book, sits down and reads—of a sudden he rises.

Yes, I'll see what can be done for this poor destitute girl. My sister, I dare say, can employ her in her domestic concerns.

[He sits down, and reads again; then takes his Eye slowly from the Book.

She can read to my sister, perhaps, and be of use that way.—But what have I to do with women's business! Here, in the country, my books are my sole occupation;
[Musing]
—books my sure solace, and refuge from frivolous cares.—Books, the calmers, as well as the instructors of the mind.

[Looks in the Book some time, then rises.

'Sdeath! I cannot read.—What is the reason I cannot read?

[Going.

[Enter **MR WILLOWEAR**.

WILLOWEAR
Well, Sir Oswin, have you seen her?

SIR OSWIN
Yes,—I have seen her.

WILLOWEAR
And what do you think of my choice?

SIR OSWIN
I think it a most imprudent one.

WILLOWEAR
Why so?

SIR OSWIN
Because she does not chuse you.

WILLOWEAR
Did she tell you so?

SIR OSWIN
Has she not proved so?

WILLOWEAR
I wish you would let me see her.

SIR OSWIN
No, by no means.
[Hastily]
I told you that if she could exculpate herself,—and in truth this has been the case.—Her promise to you, she avers, was given under the influence of fear.—She has flown to this house for protection; and I believe the laws of hospitality oblige me.—Here is your ring—But, as to the simple girl, without her own express desire, I cannot give up her.

WILLOWEAR
Well, if you say so—But, I assure you, you are the only man to whom I would confide her.

SIR OSWIN
You don't confide her.—She came hither of her own accord—and one cannot, upon reflection, turn from one's door a human creature of whatever sex, whatever age.

WILLOWEAR
And hers, to be sure, is an interesting sex, as well as a tender age.

SIR OSWIN
Which makes me the more concerned for her.

WILLOWEAR
And yet you used to be so severe, so hard upon the women.

SIR OSWIN
So I am still on women advanced in life; but one can't help having a sort of feeling for the young.

WILLOWEAR
Did she part with this ring reluctantly?

SIR OSWIN
No; with as much pleasure as if it had been yourself.

WILLOWEAR [Sighing]
So, then, I must resign all hopes of her, I find.

SIR OSWIN
That's right—And do so like a man.

WILLOWEAR [Sighing]
I must seek for some other object to divert my thoughts.—What pretty women have you hereabouts, to banish Hester from my mind?

SIR OSWIN

A number—a number.

[Eagerly.

WILLOWEAR
Who are they? What are their names?

[With indifference.

SIR OSWIN
I cannot exactly count them all over by name.
[Recollecting]
Lady Susan Courtly, however, is among them, I know.

WILLOWEAR
Is she here?

SIR OSWIN [Eagerly]
Yes.

WILLOWEAR
I once paid my addresses to Lady Susan—I have a great mind to renew them.—If she consented just now, it would take from the foolish, ridiculous figure I make, to be seen without a wife after being so near possessing one.

SIR OSWIN
She lives close by, at my uncle's.—She's on a visit there, and his house is but on the edge of my park. Come with me, and I'll show you a short cut through the grounds; And one of the pleasantest walks too—You can be there in a quarter of an hour.

[Exeunt.

ACT THE THIRD

SCENE I

A Forest, and a Ruined Cottage

LAVENSFORTH discovered stretched on a Bank, under a Tree—his Black Servant, **AMOS**, kneeling by him—an open Letter lying on the Ground.

AMOS
Master, dear master, raise your head, and speak to poor servant, poor black, who has attend you from boy in his native country, followed you to your own, and is ready to follow you all the world over. Only tell him why you no eat—why you no sleep—and why big tear roll down from your eye?
[A Pause]

Master, why you left lodgings in village, and taken this poor hut in wild forest? House not fit even for blacks—No one live near—none but the birds.—Ah, forget! This letter he threw down, brought the bad news, that breaks his heart.

[Takes the Letter from the Ground, and reads.

Unhappy man,—in all things unhappy—your daughter Hester, I fear is lost to you for ever. She eloped from my care on the very day your packet arrived; and under such circumstances, that, perhaps, I may never hear of her again. If I do, I will certainly send her the letter you enclosed for her in mine. Yours,

R. Ashdale.

Hester, that is his daughter's name; often he talks of her when in my country. Hester—poor Hester!

LAVENSFORTH [Starting, and raising his Head]
Who said "Poor Hester!" Ah! poor! for she lost her mother at her birth, and her father, when she first began to know and love him. Did any one speak her name, or was it my imagination?

[Rises.

AMOS
It was I said, Hester.

LAVENSFORTH
Wherefore?

AMOS
Because I know that name well; You so often spoke it in your sleep, while in hot countries I watched to fan you.

LAVENSFORTH
Ah! my dreams have been happier than my waking hours; for them I passed with her.

AMOS
No, master, no; Your dreams sometimes unhappy; sometimes you start.—You angry in your sleep; You call for gun, for sword—You speak another name, not kind, as you speak Hester.

LAVENSFORTH
I speak of Oswin, then, in my dreams.

AMOS
Ay, that's the name.

LAVENSFORTH
Of him, who has stripped me of every good I once possessed. Amos, I have a heart formed to love, and to hate, in the extremes—My daughter and this Oswin have, for thirteen years, shared it between them; to the one, the tenderest affection; to the other, deadly hatred. And now, that I have no longer a child, on whom to bestow my love, hate is the sole possessor of my bosom. But I will root it out.

AMOS
Do, master, do.

LAVENSFORTH
I have no daughter, for whose sake, now, I should retain my rage, and I will rid myself of it.

AMOS
You will forgive?

LAVENSFORTH
I will. There is, however, but one way left, by which I can forgive Sir Oswin, and I will avail myself of that one. I will fix my dagger in his heart, and bear him malice no longer.

AMOS
Have duel?

LAVENSFORTH
No; from that redress, years ago, I was restrained; and the only friends I ever had on earth, are bound in penalties so large, to insure my forbearance, that I must steal upon him. Amos, invention, plot, cunning, disguise, and secrecy must be employed, even to procure such a meeting. But then, Oswin, on my knees, I vow your destruction, as you have effected mine.
[Rises]
But my revenge shall be mercy, compared to yours. I will not stab your fame:—I'll only sheathe my poniard in your breast.—I will not alienate your friends, as you have done mine; but they shall follow you with lamentation to the grave.

AMOS
Master, me commit that sin, not you. Me black, who been often wounded by white man, let me wound in return; then sail to my own country, and leave master still good man—no fear—no guilt.

LAVENSFORTH
You presume to complete my designs?—Avenge my wrongs? Know your distance!

[Then inattentive to him, as he has been through all the Scene, but where he particularly addressed him.

Good fortune might have softened my mind, and driven out all impressions of revenge: But—
[In Tears]
—the many ills which have succeeded his ambitious prosecution! my child! a female child, left without parents, the heaviest ill of all.—His courting popularity at my expense! his art of eloquence, which, in a boy, had power to crush a man. Of the miseries produced by talents so perverted, he shall feel his share:—He shall find I am not less cruel now, than when I ruled in my government;—that exile has not softened me. The young enthusiast but accused me of acts of despotism; he shall prove, in his dying moments, there is not a crime too black for my accomplishment.

AMOS
Good master, no more grief, but return to lodgings in the village.

LAVENSFORTH
No house shall shelter me, but this ruined cottage; no bed shall rest my limbs, and rack my brain, till I have revenged my wrongs.

[Goes into the Cottage, returns, and speaks at the Door.

My enemy, this Sir Oswin Mortland, has a seat, not more than ten miles distant; Mortland Abbey. Inquire of the peasants what road he frequents; whether he passes this way to the next town; whether he hunts, or shoots, or strolls in his park of an evening: Gain all the intelligence you can. Revenge is dear to men of your complexion, even more than to those of mine: Therefore, I depend, not alone on your fidelity and secrecy, but on your eager exertions.

AMOS
Oh, master! only kind master I ever had! I would die for your content.

LAVENSFORTH
Live, and execute my orders.

[**LAVENSFORTH** retires into the Cottage, and **AMOS** into the Forest.

SCENE II

A Saloon at Lord Danberry's, with Folding Doors into a Garden.

Enter **LORD DANBERRY**.

LORD DANBERRY [Looking towards the Garden]
There they are! there they are! Now would I give a hundred pounds, to know what Lady Susan and Sir Oswin are saying to each other. They have been together exactly five minutes and a half by my stop-watch.—He has certainly begun the subject by this time; but I can't know any thing of their conversation unless I join them; and that would be a pity, for it would interrupt them. I found it difficult to drag him to my house, and more so to persuade him to wait on her in the garden. Then away I slipt, and now he is alone with her, he will be caught at once. He must speak now—here they come! here they come!—Yes, they are coming into this very room, as I live: Now he must break the matter without delay, and my wishes are completed.

[Exit.

[Enter **SIR OSWIN** and **LADY SUSAN COURTLY**, from the Garden.—As he and **LADY SUSAN** sit down,

SIR OSWIN
Lady Susan, I am a peculiar man, but a plain man: my peculiarity consists in my plainness. I am under the greatest obligations to my uncle, who bestowed on me an education, and tutors, who made me reflect; reflect particularly on my own passions, inclinations, faults, and failings. In return for his care, I wish to obey him in all his commands; but serious, sober, I'm afraid I may say, sullen habits, have ever been predominant with me; and I never was, and, perhaps, never shall be, in love.

LADY SUSAN
Sir Oswin, your candour is so bewitching, it is impossible to resist its force. I have been accustomed to so much flattery, such adulation from men of the world, whose ardour, I am sure, meant nothing; that I cannot help believing,—your apathy means a great deal.

SIR OSWIN
You may deceive yourself, Lady Susan.

LADY SUSAN
And so may you, Sir Oswin.

SIR OSWIN
As I observed before, madam, self-examination has been my daily practice.

LADY SUSAN
Perhaps you examine so frequently, that you weary penetration; and a passer-by, knows you better, than you know yourself.

SIR OSWIN
That observation, madam, might hold true of a lady and her looking-glass; but not of a man and his faults.

LADY SUSAN
He must, however, be a very bad man, Sir Oswin, who sees his faults thus daily, yet does not amend them.

SIR OSWIN
He will, at least, endeavour to shun all trials that he thinks beyond his strength; and, in that spirit, I fear a married life.

LADY SUSAN
Marriage may be productive of some faults; but, surely, 'tis a soil fit for the cultivation of every virtue.

SIR OSWIN
Patience, I believe, may thrive there.

LADY SUSAN
But what do you say of the growth of conjugal love?

SIR OSWIN
That conjugal hate too frequently chokes it.

LADY SUSAN
I long to convince you of your mistake.

SIR OSWIN [Rising]

Madam, to end the argument, and not to make my visit tedious;—If you think you can be happy with a man so much older than yourself, who reads all the day, and half the night—whose temper is not good—who is easily put out of humour—

LADY SUSAN
That I never am; therefore my good temper will make your fretful one, of no harm to either of us.

SIR OSWIN
I'll say no more, madam; My uncle will tell you the rest of my imperfections.

LADY SUSAN
They must all appear trivial, Sir Oswin, when compared with that sincerity which discloses them.

[He bows.

I am, you shall find, sir, as peculiar, as plain spoken for a woman, as you are for a man. I scorn, like you, to follow common modes and manners, which my own opinion, or my own convenience disapproves; And while you have the singular frankness to tell me to my face, that you had rather not have me for a wife, I will have the same simple candour, and confess—that, of all things, I should like you for a husband.

SIR OSWIN
Good morning, Lady Susan.

LADY SUSAN
Good morning, Sir Oswin.

[As **SIR OSWIN** is going, Enter **LORD DANBERRY**.

LORD DANBERRY
Stay, my dear nephew, stay; Nothing on earth could give me greater joy than to be present at this interview: So, prolong it a little for my sake.

SIR OSWIN
I am afraid of intruding.

LADY SUSAN
Not at all, Sir Oswin. The man who has honoured me with the offer of his hand—

LORD DANBERRY
Then the offer is made, and you are his betrothed wife?

LADY SUSAN
As you have previously told me, my lord: but Sir Oswin has said very little.

LORD DANBERRY
Talking is not his talent; that is, talking to you women; for he thinks that would be encroaching on your privileges: when he speaks, 'tis for nothing less than the good of the nation.

LADY SUSAN
If I may judge of his other virtues by his humility, he will make the best husband in the world; for he assures me he shall be the worst.

SIR OSWIN
My uncle knows, madam—

LORD DANBERRY
I know that you are a good man, and, therefore, will make a good husband. You were the most dutiful son—you are an affectionate nephew—a good brother—a staunch friend—a friend to the orphan; for that pretty girl, whom you have just taken into your house, how kindly I saw you look on her!

LADY SUSAN
What pretty girl?

SIR OSWIN
A child, madam; a mere child.

LORD DANBERRY
Nothing the worse for being young; nor the worse for her beauty.

LADY SUSAN
Is she so beautiful, Sir Oswin?

SIR OSWIN
I was going to say, I had never looked at her; but I did—I did.

LADY SUSAN
Who is she? What's her name?

SIR OSWIN
I never asked: she was friendless, I heard.

LORD DANBERRY
And well she might; for she ran from all her friends, and the man to whom she was going to be married, at the church door.

LADY SUSAN
What a surprising occurrence!

SIR OSWIN
And yet I can conceive it might happen.

LORD DANBERRY
But the best of the story is, (as her guardian has written just now to Mr. Willowear,) she persuaded a second lover of her's to hire the post chaise for her escape from the first, on a promise she would go off

with him; but, as they were stepping into the vehicle, she pretended to swoon, and, while the poor man ran for a smelling bottle, she drove away, and left both her lovers in the same deserted state.

SIR OSWIN
Can this be fact?

LORD DANBERRY
Mr. Willowear but now showed it under her guardian's hand; who adds, he believes she will, in the end, prefer this second lover.

SIR OSWIN [Anxiously]
Who is he? What's his name?

LORD DANBERRY
He did not say.

SIR OSWIN
'Tis fit, however, I should search into the truth of this story, before she remains longer in my house.

[Going.

LORD DANBERRY
Nay, don't put yourself in a passion with her; don't go home on purpose—don't leave Lady Susan.

SIR OSWIN
If it be proper to order Hester away, the sooner she knows my will the better.

LORD DANBERRY
Then send a message to your sister; my own man shall take it, and see her safe off, at once.

SIR OSWIN
No; she shall not go till she has received from my own lips, the reproof she deserves, for having dared to come.

LORD DANBERRY
Why, then Lady Susan and I will go with you. Lady Susan, we'll go with my nephew.

[Enter **SERVANT**.

SERVANT
Mr. Willowear.

[Exit **SERVANT**.

[Enter **MR WILLOWEAR**.

SIR OSWIN
Pray, Mr. Willowear,—But, no,—I'll talk to Hester herself.

[Going.

LORD DANBERRY
Nephew, nephew!—one word.

[They talk together.

WILLOWEAR
Lady Susan, I did myself the honour of waiting on your ladyship yesterday; but you were not within.

LADY SUSAN
O! yes—I think they told me so.

WILLOWEAR
Hearing your ladyship was in this part of the world, I came to confess my shame. I knew it would be impossible to conceal it from you, and I wished to be the first to announce it. I have been slighted, in the most public manner, by one of your sex, to whom I paid my addresses, in consequence of their having been rejected by you.

LADY SUSAN
She used you rightly, if you only made your offer on my refusal.

WILLOWEAR
But, then, are not you bound to take pity on me now, if my attachment to you has ruined me with every other woman?

LORD DANBERRY [Impetuously]
You don't mean this seriously, I hope, Mr. Willowear; because Sir Oswin—

LADY SUSAN
My lord, let Sir Oswin speak for himself.

SIR OSWIN
I can't think of interrupting my uncle, madam.

LORD DANBERRY [In a positive and angry Tone]
Why, then, Mr. Willowear, this lady is engaged to Sir Oswin, and will shortly be his wife; and let me tell you, sir—

SIR OSWIN
My lord, how can you be so warm?

LORD DANBERRY
Sir Oswin, how can you be so cold?

SIR OSWIN
My lord—

LADY SUSAN
Don't interrupt your uncle, Sir Oswin.

WILLOWEAR
I beg ten thousand pardons; but it was Sir Oswin, who first told me Lady Susan was here. And I understood—

LORD DANBERRY
You can't misunderstand any longer now, sir.

WILLOWEAR
Upon any honour, I think I do—for Sir Oswin's going to be united to Lady Susan, is the most surprising!—Sir Oswin!—who has always protested there was no such thing as love.

SIR OSWIN
But I never denied there was matrimony.

[Exit **SIR OSWIN**.

LADY SUSAN
What a prospect for me in the marriage state! But I'll be revenged for his chilling insolence; and nothing on earth shall make me resign him.

LORD DANBERRY
That's right, my proud woman!

WILLOWEAR
Lady Susan, I admire your spirit so much, that I have a great mind to say,—nothing on earth shall make me resign you.

LORD DANBERRY
Would you supplant Sir Oswin, Mr. Willowear? Is it friendly?

WILLOWEAR
'Tis fashionable.

LADY SUSAN
Will you, my lord, insist on Sir Oswin's promise, given to you?

LORD DANBERRY
I will;—I do insist upon it.

LADY SUSAN
Then I'll force him to marry me.

WILLOWEAR
Do—and force him to love you too.

LADY SUSAN
So I will. For I'll bear his cruelty with so much good humour, that, unless his heart be more frozen than his manners, it shall beat with warmth to me.

[Exit.

WILLOWEAR [Following her]
Stay, Lady Susan—take pity on the only man who loves you—do not drive me to despair.

[Turns hastily.

My lord, can you tell me of any other woman whom you think I could love?

LORD DANBERRY
Why, upon my word, Mr. Willowear, it seems, as if you could love every woman you saw.

WILLOWEAR
I own I am not difficult; but, I find they are so.

LORD DANBERRY
My advice is, pursue Hester—try to redeem her; and, if you do not succeed—
[Considering]
I have just thought of the very female, who will exactly suit you.

WILLOWEAR
Of perfectly good character, I hope?

LORD DANBERRY
The nicest.

WILLOWEAR
Family?

LORD DANBERRY
The very best in the country.

WILLOWEAR
Fortune?

LORD DANBERRY
Better than Lady Susan's.

WILLOWEAR
When will you introduce me?

[Eagerly.

LORD DANBERRY
I'll mention the subject to her first, and settle every thing between you both, as I have settled between Sir Oswin and Lady Susan.

WILLOWEAR
But that alliance does not appear to be quite settled yet—I hope you will be more successful for me.

LORD DANBERRY
I'll be successful for you all. But, before I undertake your affairs, you must come with me to Sir Oswin's, and try to regain Hester.

WILLOWEAR
My lord, I am of an easy, complying, satisfied disposition. I am willing to marry Hester; or Lady Susan; or the unknown female you propose; or, if she does not like me, some other. I am not one of those, who think "great care must be taken in the choice of a wife, that she may prove a blessing."

LORD DANBERRY
No, say with me—great care must be taken how you treat a wife, and she will certainly be a blessing.

[Exeunt.

ACT THE FOURTH

SCENE I

An Apartment at Sir Oswin Mortland's.

Enter **ROBERTS**, **JAMES**, **HARRY**, and **JOHN**, Servants to Sir Oswin.

ROBERTS
Do you run to the terrace, and see for her.

[Exit **JOHN**.

Go you, and see if she's in the drawing-room.

[Exit **JAMES**.

And run you into the park.

[Exit **HARRY**.

[Enter **MRS SARAH MORTLAND**.

MRS MORTLAND
What is the matter? What's all this confusion about?

ROBERTS
I thought Miss Hester was here, ma'am.

MRS MORTLAND
And what did you want with her?

ROBERTS
Sir Oswin is just returned from Lord Danberry's, and desires to see her directly. He seems not very well pleased at something.

MRS MORTLAND
You mean, he is in an ill humour.

ROBERTS [In a Whisper]
He's coming, ma'am.

[Exit.

[Enter **SIR OSWIN**.

SIR OSWIN [In Anger]
Where is your protègée, your companion, your innocent girl? Where's Hester?

MRS MORTLAND
And now, give me leave to ask a question. Where is your elder sister? For one would suppose she was not within hearing.

SIR OSWIN
She lost her consequence, when she listened to the tale of an impostor.

MRS MORTLAND
What has thus changed you on a sudden? We passed yesterday in comfort all together—and your attention to this poor girl, was remarkable.

SIR OSWIN
Who remarked it?

MRS MORTLAND
Myself—Lord Danberry. However, do you want to see her?

SIR OSWIN
I do.

MRS MORTLAND
Then I'll send her to you—
[Aside]
—and glad of the opportunity to get away.

[Exit.

SIR OSWIN [In Anger]
Women!—women!—women!—
[Altering his Tone, but still angry]
Woman! woman! woman!—
[In greater Anger still]
Woman!

[Enter HESTER.

[His Voice softens as he beholds her, and he tenderly pronounces 'woman!'

[HESTER courtesies, and appears timid.

SIR OSWIN [With a subdued agitation]
If they were slight faults that you had committed, you would see me in anger;—as it is—as your indiscreet conduct has been flagrant—you find me impressed only with concern, that I am compelled to turn from my habitation, a friendless young woman, who has implored my protection—and afflicted—deeply afflicted—to behold depravity in one, who gave no warning to the eye, no caution to the ear, nor even to the understanding, to beware of her arts.

HESTER
Am I artful? If you say so, I suppose I am; but, indeed, I did not know it.

SIR OSWIN
Were not those arts, by which you deceived two lovers?

HESTER
O! lovers! Yes, I have made fools of two lovers. But I had a right to do so—for they wanted to make a fool of me.

SIR OSWIN
How so?

HESTER
Why, Mrs. Ashdale, my guardian's wife, and all the elderly ladies, that visited her, constantly said to me, "Hester, never mind what the men say; they are deceitful, and always speak falsehood to young women." So, I put no trust in them, nor they, I hope, in me.

SIR OSWIN
One honourable man was on the point of marrying you, when you ran away.

HESTER
I thought it was better to run away before marriage, than after.

SIR OSWIN

But you broke your promise.

HESTER
Not my marriage promise—for that I am resolved to keep, marry when I will: which makes me so afraid of giving it.

SIR OSWIN [Aside]
That is from the heart.

HESTER
Have you any thing more to say against me?

SIR OSWIN
Who was he that effected your escape?

HESTER
I did not know him for a lover; but trusted him only as a friend, to procure me a chaise; when, on a sudden, thinking me in his power, he wanted to come away with me. So, I feigned illness, to leave him behind, too.—Any more reproaches?

SIR OSWIN
Numberless. You have, in every instance, conducted yourself with so much imprudence, indecorum,—that I am offended you should have dared to come into this house.

HESTER
Ay, now I hope you are speaking falsehood, as all the men do to young women.

SIR OSWIN
I speak falsehood!

HESTER
Only to women—don't be angry—I mean only to women.

SIR OSWIN
I speak truth to every one; and it is true that you have forfeited my good opinion, and all that favourable impression, which your appearance first made on me.

HESTER
Did I make a favourable impression on you? Oh! I am so proud of it!

SIR OSWIN [Confounded]
I—I give you leave to conceive this as a falsehood.

HESTER
No:—you always "speak truth;" and I will believe this true, because I should be sorry to have it otherwise: for then, what would become of me? where should I go?

SIR OSWIN

Return to those, who reared you from your infancy.

HESTER
No, no, never.

SIR OSWIN
Marry, and you'll have a home.

HESTER
Why do you bid me marry? I am told that you don't like to marry any more than I do. But, sir,—is not this a fair proposal?—I'll marry, if you will.

SIR OSWIN [Starting]
Mr. Willowear, would you marry?

HESTER
No; I'll make my own choice.

SIR OSWIN [Agitated]
And whom would you choose?

HESTER
I'll tell you, if you'll promise I shall have him.

SIR OSWIN [After a Pause]
Hear me, Hester—I sent for you, to upbraid, to reproach you—to show my displeasure—my resentment; but, you talk so differently from all the world besides, that—that—I have no words to give in exchange for yours, but such as I feel disinclined to utter.

HESTER
Are they cruel, or kind words, that you suppress?

SIR OSWIN
I hardly know their meaning.

HESTER
Speak them, and I'll explain them.

SIR OSWIN
No, no;—no explanations.
[He walks about in Disquietude.

HESTER [After a Pause]
And now, if my examination is over, am I to stay or go?

SIR OSWIN
I am not determined.

HESTER
Shall I determine for you?

SIR OSWIN [After a Struggle]
I confess, since the conversation which has just passed between us, I feel a reluctance to say those harsh things, I meant to do, before I saw you.

HESTER
We feel something alike; for, before we met, I intended to say a thousand kind things, to persuade you to let me remain here; but the moment I saw you, I felt reluctant to speak them.

SIR OSWIN
It is not discreet in a woman, to speak with kindness to men.

HESTER
Not if they speak kindly to her: but when they are cross, like you, she may be kind with safety.

SIR OSWIN
Hester, with all your faults, I feel an interest in your welfare. And when I say, I feel for another's happiness, I am not interested slightly. You have been imprudent, and I have censured you—but, in the hope my censure may have influence, I commence, from this hour, a friendship—a sincere friendship, for you. Remain in this house while it suits your convenience, and reveal to me all your heavy sorrows, all your anxious troubles—my power shall protect, my sympathy shall console you.

HESTER [After pausing a little Time, impressed with Surprise]
Oh! this serious, this solemn profession of regard for me, has ruined all my hopes, all my expectations!

SIR OSWIN
How so? How?

HESTER
Because it forces me to be serious and solemn with you. While you were proud, I could treat you lightly;—while you were angry, I did not regard you;—while you were severe, I could laugh at you. But now you are generous, humble, mild, I cannot impose on you—cannot deceive you longer.

SIR OSWIN
Deceive me! In what? Don't I know all your faults?

HESTER
Not half of them.

SIR OSWIN
Have a care! you may yet lose me as your friend.

HESTER

I may—Oh, I must!—I know I must!—I shall not make my confession unwarily; for I know, the moment you have heard it we shall part, never to meet again. Yet, I had rather it should be so, than live with you every day, and be ashamed to lift up my eyes in your presence.

SIR OSWIN [Alarmed]
Why ashamed? Why are you to be excluded from the right, which every one who is friendless has to my protection?

HESTER [Trembling]
Because I am the unhappy child—of the unfortunate Lavensforth.

SIR OSWIN [Starting with Horror]
My enemy! my mortal enemy! The man, who has threatened, who has repeatedly sworn, to take my life!

[She falls gradually on her Knees, as he speaks thus to himself.

The man, whom my rigour has irritated to this phrenzy! Ay, Oswin, reason for your foe, as well as for yourself.—Act, too, for him.
[To her]
I do not discard you for your father's sake; and you shall be still nearer to me for your own.
[Raises her]
Nay, why this trembling, this tremour?

HESTER
Wherefore am I thus impelled, thus forced, to love the man who was my father's enemy?

SIR OSWIN
If I continued such, I would not offend you with the offer of my services. But time and reflection have made me doubt of his demerits, and my own justice in arraigning him.

HESTER
Ah! do you say so? Do I hear there is a doubt—a supposition—a hope, that my dear father has been unjustly accused?

SIR OSWIN
From his open, his once professed enemy, his daughter shall receive his character; and before she blesses—honours—my abode with her future residence, shall know—that I respected the man whom I impeached: for esteem was not incompatible with that peculiar suit I preferred against him. And, now, while compassion suggests numerous excuses for his past deeds—and impartiality obliges me to reprove my own,—do you, his representative, accept all the retribution I can offer for measures too severe, perhaps, in the cause of political warfare.

[He takes her Hand, and embraces her tenderly.

[Enter **LORD DANBERRY**.

LORD DANBERRY

Ah! what! my rigid, reserved nephew, with a fair maid in his arms! Oh! you can unbend, I find, serene and mighty potentate, when no one is by.
[To **HESTER**]
Madam, Mr. Willowear is in the next room, come to claim you—you blush!—but never mind—I won't tell—mum!—For my part, Sir Oswin, I am rather glad to see that you can get a pretty girl in a corner; for if you do one, you soon may another; and Lady Susan, perhaps, has no cause to despair. Mum!—hush!—I won't say a word—only I must laugh—ha! ha! ha! Is this the lesson you came home to give the poor orphan? Ha! ha! ha!

SIR OSWIN
My lord, you—

LORD DANBERRY
No excuses—'tis all very well—only give a little of your kindness to Lady Susan.—I thought it would show itself at last!

HESTER
Sir—

LORD DANBERRY
No excuses, my dear—I forgive—no excuses.

SIR OSWIN
My lord, you put me in a rage!

LORD DANBERRY
Ay, the cold fit has been gone some time.

HESTER
My lord, Sir Oswin was so kind—

LORD DANBERRY
You need not tell me. I saw how kind he was!

SIR OSWIN
Hold!—that lady must not be insulted—she is under my protection.

LORD DANBERRY
Well, this is leaping from the "freezing point" to "fever heat" at once! One moment in Lapland, the next under the torrid zone! I wish you joy, young lady, of this your third lover; but, perhaps, I should not be so content, if a fourth was not behind.

SIR OSWIN
A fourth lover!

LORD DANBERRY
Yes; her guardian has just sent a postchaise (at least a messenger, who was to procure one, if he found her here) to take her to a fourth lover, who may, perhaps, extinguish your burning flame.

HESTER
Oh, Sir Oswin, save me from my guardian, and his tyranny!

SIR OSWIN
But if your guardian possesses any power, any authority, I have no legal right to withhold you.

[Sighing.

HESTER
But, you may have.

LORD DANBERRY
There,—she speaks as plain English, as ever I heard a woman utter.

SIR OSWIN
Plain English is what so few of the English do speak,—

[Enter **MRS SARAH MORTLAND**, with two Letters in her Hand.

MRS MORTLAND
Hester,—

[When **MRS MORTLAND** calls out "Hester," **LORD DANBERRY** passes by **SIR OSWIN** towards **HESTER**]

Here is a letter for you, which came inclosed in this to me; and there's a person from your guardian, who begs to see you instantly.

[**MRS SARAH MORTLAND** retires, reading her own Letter.

HESTER [Looks at the Address of her Letter with surprise, and hissing it, exclaims apart]
My father's hand! Oh, unexpected happiness!

[Exit hastily.

SIR OSWIN
Her guardian! What can all this mean?

LORD DANBERRY [Apart]
I must have an eye upon this girl. She must not belong to my family;

[Looking suspiciously at **SIR OSWIN**.

I must watch her.

[Exit, following **HESTER**.

MRS MORTLAND [Advancing to **SIR OSWIN**]

You are absorbed in thought! May I ask what is the subject of your reflections?

SIR OSWIN
A confused mass! I am living in this old world, and yet a new one seems to have broken upon me, to make me as a stranger to all around.

MRS MORTLAND
Shall I inform you, where you are?

SIR OSWIN
It would be an act of charity.

MRS MORTLAND
But will you take it charitably?

SIR OSWIN
Yes.

MRS MORTLAND
You are—in love.

SIR OSWIN [Starts]
What makes you think so?

MRS MORTLAND
Don't you feel so?

SIR OSWIN
No,—no,—no,—let's hope not,—no—no.

MRS MORTLAND
You have all the symptoms.

SIR OSWIN
No—no.—And who made you a judge?

MRS MORTLAND
That is a secret I shall keep to myself.

SIR OSWIN
Women, to be sure, know every thing.

MRS MORTLAND
The reason is—women feel every thing. Men's perception lies only in the head; ours comes from the heart. Brother, the two sexes are thus contrasted—Sensibility gives us wisdom, but takes it away from you men. When man is governed by his heart, he's less than woman—and we are the lords of the creation.

SIR OSWIN
In this case neither my heart nor head convicts me.

MRS MORTLAND
No; for they dupe you.

SIR OSWIN [Frightened]
Do you speak in earnest?

MRS MORTLAND
Most assuredly.

SIR OSWIN [Trembling and reaching a Chair]
Why, then, if I am in love,—if it must be so,—I may as well submit.

[Sits down.

It is vain, I suppose, to contend with my passion, and I must give myself up to my fate? Hard fate? after all my studies, my researches, my meditations, my zeal for the public good!—And what am I to do in respect to Lady Susan?

MRS MORTLAND
You must tell her you prefer another.

SIR OSWIN [In the same distressed tone]
If I told her I was married to another, she would say she liked me the better for it.
[Recovering his spirits]
Hester is different from her: she has a horror of the marriage state.

MRS MORTLAND
So, from the self-same antipathy arises this dangerous sympathy. But as I allured you into her power, it is in my duty to snatch you from it. This letter was just now brought me from her guardian.

SIR OSWIN [Takes the Letter and reads]
Madam, do me the favour to give Hester the inclosed, the contents of which she is bound to keep secret. All I shall add is, that you can, upon no pretence whatever, detain her longer, when I assure you, that this inclosed letter comes to her from one, who (as I have acquainted him with her flight) must be in the deepest despair till he sees her; as there is between them a mutual and indissoluble affection.
A mutual affection!
[Rising]
Yes, I observed her delight on seeing the hand which directed her letter.—'Tis true, she has a secret lover, and I will search him out, or—

MRS MORTLAND
Now this is jealousy.

SIR OSWIN [Starting]
Jealous; do you accuse me of love, and then dare to add jealousy?

MRS MORTLAND
They follow naturally.

SIR OSWIN
Why, then, welcome all the tumultuous passions at once; for I find my heart is as unable to resist the one as the other.

[Throws himself into a Chair.

MRS MORTLAND
Ah! I foresaw—

SIR OSWIN
Why did you not caution me, then? why did you not tell me? I felt no fears—I despised all danger—
[Starts up]
Why did you ever bring her to my house? Or, rather, why not long since? For, till I knew her, I never knew one rapturous sensation.

[Enter **HESTER**, with a Letter in her Hand.

HESTER
I am come to take my leave of you for ever.

SIR OSWIN
Why so?

[**MRS MORTLAND** goes round to **HESTER**.

HESTER
I must not tell you why.

SIR OSWIN
And do you go by your own consent?

HESTER
I do.

SIR OSWIN
Then wherefore do you weep?

HESTER
Half these tears are for joy, half for sorrow.

SIR OSWIN
Explain.

HESTER

I dare not; but must follow my guardian's directions, and immediately set off in the carriage, which his servant, who brought this letter, is gone to procure me.

SIR OSWIN
Alone?

HESTER
All alone.

SIR OSWIN
Not an hour ago you solicited me to save you from your guardian's power.

HESTER
But I was not then acquainted with the cause, which—Oh! Sir Oswin, an impulse you know nothing of compels—and the same impulse (confident as I am in your nice honour) ties my tongue from saying what the occasion is, which calls me.—All my own actions—all my own thoughts, I confess boldly; but when I am entrusted with the thoughts and the concerns of others, I can be mute as death.

SIR OSWIN
You are going to a lover.

HESTER
No more—than I am leaving one behind.

SIR OSWIN
And if you thought, you were?—

HESTER
Have I any right to think so?

SIR OSWIN
Do you ask me seriously?

HESTER
Yes.

SIR OSWIN
Why, then, I—

[Enter **LORD DANBERRY**.

LORD DANBERRY
The chaise waits—the postillion's in a hurry.

HESTER
Oh dear! how could you interrupt what he was going to say?

LORD DANBERRY

Hear what I have to say—The chaise is at the door—'twill be dark in half an hour—no moon—the heath you have to cross is dangerous, on account of robbers—and the rivulet, at the bottom of the hill, has, probably, overflowed.

[Enter a **MAID**.

Here's your hat and cloak.—

[He takes them of her, and gives them to **HESTER**.

I sincerely wish you a good journey, and I'll hand you to the door.

[Exit **MAID**.

SIR OSWIN
No, uncle, as the danger is so great, I'll order my horse and pistols, and ride by the side of the carriage. It would not be common hospitality to suffer a female to leave my house, unprotected, through such perils as you have described.

[Taking her Hand, and going.

HESTER [In a low Voice]
You must not go with me, for the world—not for the world, Sir Oswin.

SIR OSWIN
This alarm is suspicious!—What does it mean?

HESTER
Dear Mrs. Sarah Mortland, persuade your brother—my lord do not suffer him to go with me.

SIR OSWIN
These efforts to prevent me, fix my determination.
[Aside to **MRS MORTLAND**]
To see her meeting with her lover, will be my cure at once.

[Leading her to the Door.

HESTER
I hope that, when I have passed the dangerous part of my journey, I shall have power to persuade you to return.

SIR OSWIN
Perhaps, you may.

HESTER [Aside]
If not, I must reveal to whom I am going.

LORD DANBERRY

Nephew—nephew!
[**SIR OSWIN** returns]
You had a fixed opinion there was no such passion as love.—What can you say now?

SIR OSWIN
Like other theorists, say—I was mistaken.

[Exeunt **SIR OSWIN** and **HESTER**.

LORD DANBERRY [To **MRS MORTLAND**]
Did you ever see any thing like this?

MRS MORTLAND
Yes; for this is not the first time I have seen a man in love.

[Enter **MR WILLOWEAR**.

LORD DANBERRY
My dear Willowear, did you not meet Sir Oswin, leading away in triumph your intended wife? Run after him, and take her from him; pray now do.

WILLOWEAR
No—let Hester go—and let Lady Susan go.—I am curious and impatient to see the woman you have promised me.

LORD DANBERRY
You shan't see her; nor will I reveal who she is, till you have followed Sir Oswin.

[Walks about in anger.

WILLOWEAR
Then I'll make inquiries elsewhere.

[Bows to **MRS MORTLAND**, and goes up to her.

I beg pardon, madam; but, as I have the honour to meet you in the house of Sir Oswin, I imagine you know the name of Willowear?

[She bows assent.

And know that he has met with a certain disappointment?

MRS MORTLAND
I do sir.

WILLOWEAR
I am that unfortunate lover.—Can yon, madam, give me advice how to repair my loss? Do you know any woman of reputation who will marry a man in my forsaken state.

MRS MORTLAND
Upon my word, I am so little acquainted with any, except the married women of our neighbourhood!—I assure you Mr. Willowear, I have hardly an acquaintance who is a single lady, although I am single myself.

WILLOWEAR
Are you unmarried, madam?
[To **LORD DANBERRY**, aside]
Who is this lady? I was never introduced to her.

LORD DANBERRY
She is Sir Oswin's sister—my niece—and the very woman I mentioned for your wife.
[Having viewed **MRS MORTLAND** earnestly]
My wife! my wife!

LORD DANBERRY
No fear of running away from the church door, there.

WILLOWEAR
Marry her!—I should be the jest of all my acquaintance.

LORD DANBERRY
That you will be, at any rate.

WILLOWEAR
Mine is a desperate case.

LORD DANBERRY
And, to tell you the truth, I don't believe that even she would accept you.

WILLOWEAR
Now you pique me to make the offer.

[Goes to her.

Madam, you are Mrs. Sarah Mortland, I find.

[She courtesies.

If I thought you would pardon what I am inclined to utter—

MRS MORTLAND
Pray speak out, sir.

WILLOWEAR
Will you accept a man, slighted by all your sex?

MRS MORTLAND
Would you marry a woman, who has been slighted by all yours?

LORD DANBERRY
To be sure:—for then you can't laugh at each other.

MRS MORTLAND
If you could, Mr. Willowear, marry such a woman, I give you in reply—that at my time of life, I feel for every man the same disregard, the men all felt for me in my younger days.

[Exit.

WILLOWEAR [Confounded]
What can I do now, my lord? Will you—

LORD DANBERRY
No—I can do no more—After being refused by a maiden lady of fifty, all hope is over.

[Exit **LORD DANBERRY**.

WILLOWEAR
Nay, hear me, my lord.—Oh! that I had but Sir Oswin's aversion to matrimony.

[Exit.

ACT THE FIFTH

SCENE I

The Forest and Cottage

Moonlight.

Enter **LAVENSFORTH**.

LAVENSFORTH
How seldom do we taste the goods, which nature bestows, till we are deprived of those that are the work of art! To see the sun set, and the moon rise, is to me, robbed of every other pastime, sublime amusement! And were fortune now to shower on me all its wealth, and other hoarded blessings, still I should ever think—Hark! what noise?—Amos, returning from the village!—perhaps with letters.—The thought of news makes me shudder; for 'tis so many years since I have received welcome tidings!—Still I send, and long for letters.—But, now, what intelligence can they bring me, except the confirmation of my Hester's loss.—Hark! again;—That sound was like a groan!—No;—my own dark designs, my own black determinations, haunt me, and, in every whisper of the wind through these lofty oaks, I hear the cry of murder.

SIR OSWIN [From the Wood]
Ho! ho! Cottagers, lend assistance!

LAVENSFORTH [Calling out]
Who's there in distress? Amos, is it you? Speak again, that I may know which way the sound—

[Enter **SIR OSWIN**, pale, and near fainting.

SIR OSWIN
Good friend, a villain on the road has fired at me.

LAVENSFORTH [Going towards him]
Ha! who's that? Who are you? You are wounded, sir; lean on me—Come into this cottage. Let me bind your wounds.

[Tearing a Neckcloth from his own Neck.

Then haste for other assistance, and raise the village in pursuit of the robber.

SIR OSWIN
He is fled; I have rode a mile, at least, since I received my wound; for my horse took fright at the report of the piece, and I had no power over him, till he was stopped by this wood.

LAVENSFORTH
If you can walk into the cottage, it will be better than—

SIR OSWIN
There is a lady in a carriage, with whom I was in company, whose safety is more important to me than my own.—She was under my protection.—Lead me into the house; then, my good friend, go in search of her; silence her fears, and order the postboy to drive hither—he can take me home.

LAVENSFORTH
Here is, in this hut, a kind of couch, on which you may rest, when I have bound up your wound: I will then instantly do as you have directed. Lean on me; I can support you—Your blood flows fast. Do not talk, I charge you—it will exhaust you quite; But lean on me—lean on me—lean on me.

[Exit, drawing **SIR OSWIN** gently into the Cottage.

[Enter **AMOS**, in Fright and Terror—A Firelock in his Hand.

AMOS
Master! master! Where is he?
[Looks slightly into the Cottage Window, and about]
Cannot find him! away—is not to be found—I, left to feel joy—
[Reflecting]
—and sorrow alone!
[Trembling]

Ah! cannot bear, alone.—Master—master.—Come; I happy with you—but what, what do, if ever left alone?

[Enter **LAVENSFORTH**, from the Cottage.

LAVENSFORTH
What's all this talking! Fly instantly for the village surgeon.—Here is a gentleman within, has been wounded by some villain, who fired at him on the road.

AMOS [Starting]
Here? here?

LAVENSFORTH
Yes, here.
[With expression of Joy, and savage Fury]
It is Sir Oswin!
[**LAVENSFORTH** starts]
It is Sir Oswin.

LAVENSFORTH
You speak falsehood.

AMOS
Master, it is he.

LAVENSFORTH
No; such joy, such triumph, was never meant for me. Yet the sound pleases me—repeat it—say again, it is he.

AMOS
I know it. As I, returning from the village—this gun in my hand, which had lately borrowed—heard carriage stop on road, and postillion inquire his way—I answered to him—on which—lady from chaise-window said to gentleman on horseback—"Now, Sir Oswin, you go no further." I start at that name—went close to horses' side, and asked, if he was Sir Oswin Mortland, of Mortland Abbey. He answered, "Yes." My hand, before my thought, caught trigger of my gun, and—
[Trembling]
His horse ran away.—I came home.

LAVENSFORTH
Strike a light.

[Exit **AMOS** into the Cottage.

I'll look at him as he reclines on his couch—I shall know him.

[A Light appears at the Cottage Window, **AMOS** re-enters.

I have cause to know him.

[**LAVENSFORTH** goes into the Cottage.

AMOS
Ah! I again alone! Nobody to speak—all to think—thoughts bad company—good company once. Oh! I cannot, cannot live, if I am alone.

[Enter **LAVENSFORTH** from the Cottage.

LAVENSFORTH
'Tis he! 'tis he! the lineaments of his face are neither altered by time, nor the loss of blood. The man who has injured me bears the same features, thank Providence! as in the days of his malignant triumph. There can be no mistake; my eye, my heart, my very soul, recognizes the man. Ah! never more will I arraign just fate, who now has sent my worst enemy under my roof,

[Takes out a Dagger.

—and wounded to my hand!
[Starts]
Under my roof, and wounded to my hand!—why then, I must not harm a hair of his head!—my limbs are chained, though my revenge is raging to burst forth. Oh! would he now start up in health and vigour, surrounded by his host of friends, how boldly would I defy, and stab him to the heart. But this good fortune, these secure means of vengeance, which every skulking coward would enjoy, I, bound by a tyrannical word, called honour, dare not use.

[Enter **SIR OSWIN** from the Cottage.—Exit **AMOS**, drooping under Confusion and Remorse at his Presence.

SIR OSWIN
My good host, you have bound my wound so effectually, that the bleeding is wholly stopped; and I find my strength so well recruited by this short repose, that I hope the injury I have sustained will prove but slight. As the chaise I mentioned is not come, if you can help me to my horse, which, probably, is still about this thicket, I shall thank you.—I am Sir Oswin Mortland,
[**LAVENSFORTH** shows great Emotion]
—and, if you'll call to-morrow at my house—

[Observes **LAVENSFORTH'S** Countenance, then his Dagger.

Ah! an instrument of death in your hand! Have I been betrayed into this place? What mean you by that weapon?

LAVENSFORTH
I mean that it shall rest here,
[Putting it up]
—till you are safe at home.

SIR OSWIN

Till I am safe at home! What then?

LAVENSFORTH
Then—it shall rest, till your health is restored.

SIR OSWIN
You seem to imply some menace.—Man, who are you?

LAVENSFORTH
Your sworn, your mortal, your just enemy,—Lavensforth.

SIR OSWIN [After a Pause of Amazement]
You know the penalty under which the laws forbid my meeting you: that consideration, I am now compelled to wave, and to tell you—I have still strength and spirit to defy your threats.

[Takes Pistols from his Pockets.

Choose one of these, and take your ground.

[Takes a Pistol, then, seeming to make an Effort.

No; mean as this habitation is, proud man, it is mine; and you shall feel the weight of my protection,

[Throws away the Pistol.

—while you are within its precincts.

AMOS [Without]
A lady—a lady call for Sir Oswin.

SIR OSWIN [To **LAVENSFORTH**]
Your conduct towards me, is that of a generous foe,—

[Enter **HESTER**, leaning on **AMOS**—Exit **AMOS** into the Cottage.

—and merits a return like this,
[Goes to **HESTER**]
—to prove me worthy of it—Lavensforth, your daughter.

LAVENSFORTH
My daughter! my daughter in your care!

HESTER [Trembling]
If you are Lavensforth, I am your child.
[Kneeling]
Your once-loved Hester; most unkindly treated by those friends, with whom you trusted me, and sheltered from misfortune by—

[Looking towards **SIR OSWIN**.

LAVENSFORTH
My enemy!

HESTER
No, my father; the defender of your fame, and his own accuser, in all the conversations he has had with me, when your misfortunes were the subject. Then do not rob him of the praise due to his pity for a hapless female—who owes to him her preservation to this blissful meeting.

[Throws herself into her **FATHER'S** Arms.

LAVENSFORTH
The tender joy I feel, in thus pressing you to my bosom, hushes every murmur of resentment. "My enemy!" no;—the man who has sheltered thee, to bless my age, to sooth the rancorous passions of my soul! The man, who could preserve you, my child, from sorrow, however he has dealt with me, shall, henceforth be my friend.

HESTER
Oh, then, my father, your daughter's joy for your return is perfect.

[They embrace, and show other Tokens of Affection.

SIR OSWIN [Apart]
How poor was my exultation, whilst I urged on the ruin of this man, compared to the delight the present moment gives me!

LAVENSFORTH
No forethought, no calm consideration, could restrain me from a first embrace;—but, before I indulge too far my parental love, clear your late conduct from your guardian's accusation.

SIR OSWIN [Proudly]
Lavensforth, I would not have presented her to you, as a boon, had I not believed she was a blessing, such as I would, joyfully, receive from you.

LAVENSFORTH
My dear child! my dearest Hester! Oh! supreme must be my happiness, when I can feel it undisturbed, even by the presence of Sir Oswin.

SIR OSWIN
Suffer me to participate in your happiness! Suffer me,—
[Faintly]
Excess of interest, vehement emotions of the mind, have supplied me with strength to—but now, again—

HESTER
Ah! you have been wounded! Where is the carriage? Instantly return home.

LAVENSFORTH [Calling to **AMOS**]
Order the carriage here—to this very spot, and come back instantly.

[Exit **AMOS**.

Sir Oswin, before you and I part, you must be told—Come hither.

[Enter **AMOS**

It was this man, my servant, from whom you received your wound;—

[**AMOS** kneels, and hides his Head.

—instigated by my thirst, my plans of vengeance, but not encouraged by my most distant concurrence, or suspicion of his guilty design.

SIR OSWIN [To **AMOS**]
You have more cause to rejoice at the preservation of my life, than I have; you have escaped greater peril than myself. I'll pardon you when time shall have proved your repentance.

[**AMOS** rises, and goes into the Cottage, overwhelmed with Shame; **SIR OSWIN** is between **LAVENSFORTH** and **HESTER**, holding the Hand of each.—In Gestures, he earnestly entreats them to accompany him Home.—They go off, apparently with this Design.

SCENE II

An Apartment at Sir Oswin's.

Enter **MRS MORTLAND**, meeting **LADY SUSAN**.

MRS MORTLAND
Dear Lady Susan, I sent for you, both to console me, and share my grief! My poor brother is, perhaps, this moment breathing his last.

LADY SUSAN
Oh, heavens!

MRS MORTLAND
He went out on horseback, and was attacked by robbers: The servant, who was following at a distance, and saw him wounded, returned home, supposing his master was come back also, as he perceived him ride down a bye-road leading this way; but Sir Oswin not having returned, I fear his wounds may be mortal, and he—

LADY SUSAN
Is my lord yet informed?

MRS MORTLAND
No; and I have sent the servants all about, in vain, to seek him. Oh! my lord will die with grief when he hears the news—and I am so anxious to tell him!

[Exit in haste.

[Enter **MR WILLOWEAR**, on the opposite Side—**LADY SUSAN** turns complaisantly to him.

LADY SUSAN
How do you do, Mr. Willowear?

WILLOWEAR
To see Lady Susan smile upon me, is good fortune, so extraordinary! a smile, too, when, if report says true, her favoured lover is dying.

LADY SUSAN
The favourite lover of a woman of fashion, Mr. Willowear, has the same prerogative as a king; he never dies—there's always an immediate successor.

WILLOWEAR
Could I be that happy man!

LADY SUSAN
Yes, I'll make you heir apparent to my hand; but while Sir Oswin lives, he is its lawful sovereign.

WILLOWEAR
Nay, promise you will be mine, before you know his fate.

LADY SUSAN
No; I must delay plighting my faith, till I know whether poor Sir Oswin lives, or dies.

WILLOWEAR
That will depreciate its value. Come, give me your promise now: You can break it, you know.

LADY SUSAN
Very true; I forgot that—Then I promise.

WILLOWEAR
And thus, humbly, I take your word.

[Kneels, and kisses her Hand.

[Enter **LORD DANBERRY**.

LORD DANBERRY
Heydey! What in the name of wonder is this? More couples in corners? What do you mean, Mr. Willowear? Why, where's my nephew?

WILLOWEAR
Do you think, my lord, no man can be favoured by a lady, except your nephew?

LADY SUSAN
He is far off, my lord, and I fear, does not think of me.

LORD DANBERRY
I am a very unfortunate person! I can take no step, turn myself no way, but I intrude upon somebody's private hours. Pray, is this a concerted plan?

WILLOWEAR
How concerted? What do you mean?

LORD DANBERRY
Why, it seems to me, as if you, Mr. Willowear, with my nephew's intended bride, and he with yours, were all going down a country dance, and that each had resolved to take the wrong partner.

WILLOWEAR
I think myself happy to have any partner at all.

LADY SUSAN
And suppose we have changed partners, my lord, what then?

LORD DANBERRY
Why then, I feel myself like a blind fiddler, whose instrument has put every one in motion, only to make them change sides.

[Enter **MRS MORTLAND**.

MRS MORTLAND
Oh, my lord, I am so glad I have found you! Have not you heard that Sir Oswin has been attacked by robbers, and, perhaps, is dying?

[Enter **SIR OSWIN, LAVENSFORTH, HESTER,—SERVANTS** attending them.

LORD DANBERRY
My nephew—robbers—dying!

SIR OSWIN
No, my lord, I am still living; but my life has been in danger, and was preserved by the hospitality of this stranger.

[Showing **LAVENSFORTH**.

LORD DANBERRY
From henceforth, then, I am that stranger's friend.

SIR OSWIN

And we have agreed that I shall be so too, and he mine; though his name once indicated my direst enemy.

LORD DANBERRY
Enemy! You never had an enemy, except Lavensforth.

LAVENSFORTH
Now then, he has not one.

[Every **PERSON** shows surprise.

LORD DANBERRY
Is it possible this can be Lavensforth?

LAVENSFORTH
It is.

WILLOWEAR
And is it possible that such a reconciliation has taken place!

SIR OSWIN
Can you ask the question in a Christian country? To forgive, is the peculiar virtue, the supreme criterion of our sacred religion. We, once, were deadly foes;—This embrace—
[Embraces **LAVENSFORTH**.
—is the confession, the bold confession of our faith.

LAVENSFORTH
We have hated as men, not reflecting on man's infirmities,—but presuming to expect divine perfections, clothed in human clay.

MRS MORTLAND
To speak in the same phrase, has not this little piece of earth helped to effect the wonderful change? Is she not of the same soil with him?

[Pointing to **HESTER** and **LAVENSFORTH**.

LAVENSFORTH
She is my daughter, and was given to me by Sir Oswin, when I thought her lost.

LORD DANBERRY
I have no notion how all this has been accomplished! But that I shall learn hereafter, I suppose. And now, Mr. Lavensforth, I verily believe, that the only recompense you can make my nephew for his gift, is to return her back again.

SIR OSWIN
If you do, Lavensforth, and Hester comes willingly, I will endow her with my heart, and protect her with my life.

[LAVENSFORTH gives HESTER to SIR OSWIN.

WILLOWEAR
And will you go to church again, young lady?

HESTER
Yes; and shall remember, with more joy than ever, that I once ran away from it.

LAVENSFORTH
And now you possess all that is dear to me, Sir Oswin, what mighty compensation you have in your power, for my past afflictions!

LADY SUSAN
And will Sir Oswin stoop from his solemn, stately grandeur, to be married at last? Ha! ha! ha!

WILLOWEAR
Not only to marry, but to marry for love—Ha! ha! ha!

LADY SUSAN & WILLOWEAR
Ha! ha! ha!

SIR OSWIN
Mr. Willowear—Lady Susan—I should have apologies to make for some parts of my conduct to both of you; but I allow you the privilege of laughing at me; and I'm sure you'll think that a sufficient atonement.

WILLOWEAR
Sir Oswin, you are perfectly welcome to that lady, as Lady Susan has given me her promise to take me at last.

LADY SUSAN
But I can break it, you know, Mr. Willowear.

WILLOWEAR
But you won't, you know, Lady Susan.

LORD DANBERRY
As I said just now, you are all set to cross partners; but I consent—and pray Heaven that marriage may prove to each couple a merry tune; and none of you, ever make a false step in the dance.

MRS MORTLAND
But now, gentlemen, and ladies, don't delay, but marry to-morrow: for you are all such slippery kind of people, I'm afraid you should yet glide from each other's grasp.

SIR OSWIN
That would be a prospect of more terror to me, than ever matrimony was: For the passion I once derided, now repays itself for my scorn, and forces me thus openly to declare—That there certainty is such a tender power, such a rapturous influence, as—love—And, that every man, who feels, like me, its genuine force, should—marry.

Mrs Inchbald – A Short Biography

Elizabeth Simpson was born on 15th October 1753 at Stanningfield, near Bury St Edmunds, Suffolk. She was the eighth of nine children to John Simpson, a farmer, and his wife, Mary, née Rushbrook. The family were Roman Catholics.

Her brother was educated at school, but Elizabeth, like her sisters, was educated at home. Elizabeth also suffered from a speech impediment, a stammer.

Elizabeth's father had died when she was only eight, leaving her mother to take care of a large family. These were difficult times.

Despite the fact that she suffered from a debilitating stammer she was determined, from a very young age, to become an actress. She had loved theatre from her very first childhood visit.

As a young woman Elizabeth was tall and slender. But this beauty brought with it the many attentions of men. It was double-edged.

Elizabeth had written to the manager of the Norwich Theatre to obtain acting work. He had replied that he would welcome a visit for her to audition. For her young naïve years this seemed like a golden opportunity. However, in 1770 her family forbade her attempt to take on an acting assignment there. They had no such qualms with her brother George, who entered the acting profession.

In April 1772, Elizabeth left, without permission, for London to pursue her chosen career. Although she was successful in obtaining parts her audiences found it difficult to admire her talents given her speech impediment. However, Elizabeth was diligent and hard-working on attempting to overcome this hurdle. She spent much time concentrating on pronunciation in order to eliminate the stammer. She was known to write out the parts she wanted to perform and practice the lines to point of such familiarity that her impediment was banished. Her acting, although at times stilted, especially in monologues, gained praise for her approach, and for her well-developed characters. For the audience she came across as a real person, not just an actor performing a piece. Elizabeth would keenly study the performances of others before she herself performed.

In these early months Elizabeth was young and alone, and reportedly also suffered from the attentions of sexual predators.

In June, merely two months after arriving she accepted an offer of marriage from Joseph Inchbald, a fellow Catholic and actor. They had met before on her previous trips to London, usually to see her brother, George, acting on stage. He had written her several letters proposing marriage which she had declined. But now it seemed the most expedient way to make progress in her career.

By all accounts it was still an odd choice. Joseph was a so-so actor, and at least twice her age as well as being the father of two illegitimate sons. The marriage was to produce no children and was not the happiest of unions.

On 4th September of that year, 1772, Elizabeth and Joseph appeared for the first time together on stage in 'King Lear'. The following month they toured Scotland with the West Digges's theatre company. This was to continue for the next four years.

In 1776 they decided on a change of career and a change of country. They moved to France. Joseph would now learn to paint, and Elizabeth would study French. It was a short-lived disaster. Within a month all their funds were gone and a return to England was necessitated.

They moved to Liverpool, Canterbury and Yorkshire and acted for both the Joseph Younger's company and Tate Wilkinson's company in search of permanency and a recovery from their ill-fortune.

Completely unexpectedly Joseph died in June 1779. Despite her loss Elizabeth continued to perform across the country from Dublin to London and places in between.

In 1780, she joined the Covent Garden Company and played Bellarion in 'Philaster'.

In all Elizabeth's acting career was only moderately successful and lasted some 17 years. However, she appeared in many classical roles as well as new plays such as Hannah Cowley's 'The Belle's Stratagem'. Around the theatre she was known for upholding high moral standards. She later described having to fend off sexual advances from, among others, stage manager James Dodd and theatre manager John Taylor.

It was now in the years after her husband's death that that Elizabeth decided on a new literary path. With no attachments, and acting taking up only some of her time, she decided to write plays.

Her first play to be performed was 'A Mogul Tale or, The Descent of the Balloon', in 1784, in which she also played the leading female role of Selina. The play was premiered at the Haymarket Theatre.

'Lovers' Vows', in 1798, was based on her translation of August von Kotzebues original work and garnered both praise and complements from Jane Austen and was featured as a focus of moral controversy in her novel Mansfield Park. Although Austen's book brought more fame to Elizabeth, 'Lovers' Vows' initially ran for only forty-two nights when originally performed in 1798.

One of the things that separated Elizabeth from other contemporary playwrights was her ability to translate plays from German and French into English and to use them as a foundation. These translations were popular with the public and her talents in bringing the characters to life was instrumental in achieving this.

Her success as a playwright enabled Elizabeth to support herself and not need a new husband to carry out this role. Between 1784 and 1805 she had 19 of her comedies, sentimental dramas, and farces (many of them translations from the French) performed at London theatres, although it is thought she actually wrote between 21 and 23 in total depending on which account you think is most accurate. She is usually credited as Mrs Inchbald.

As well she wrote two novels; 'A Simple Story' was published in 1791 and once referred to as "the most elegant English fiction of the eighteenth century". 'Nature and Art' was published in 1796. Both have been constantly reprinted.

Her four-volume autobiography was destroyed before her death upon the advice of her confessor, but she left a few of her diaries.

In her later years she found time to do a considerable amount of editorial and critical work. In 1805, she decided to try being a theatre critic. This literary excursion, after the praise for her acting and more so for her writing, seemed to be a low point in her achievements. The reception to her work amongst her peer critics was low, one commented upon her ignorance of Shakespeare.

Her career from actress, to playwright and novelist was achieved in difficult times for women to accomplish such things. Indeed, whilst the theatre and its boundaries were quite strict she managed, in her novels, to explore political radicalism. Her good looks together with her passionate and fiery nature attracted a string of admirers but she never re-married. Despite her love of independence, she still desired and sought social respectability.

Mrs Elizabeth Inchbald died on 1st August 1821 in Kensington, London.

She is buried in the churchyard of St Mary Abbots. On her gravestone is written, "Whose writings will be cherished while truth, simplicity, and feelings, command public admiration."

Mrs Inchbald – A Concise Bibliography

Plays
Mogul Tale; or, The Descent of the Balloon (1784)
Appearance is against Them (1785)
I'll Tell you What (1785)
The Widow's Vow (1786)
The Midnight Hour (1787)
Such Things Are (1787)
All on a Summer's Day (1787)
Animal Magnetism (c1788)
The Child of Nature (1788)
The Married Man (1789)
Next Door Neighbours (1791)
Everyone has his Fault (1793)
To Marry, or not to Marry (1793)
The Wedding Day (1794)
Wives as They Were and Maids as They Are (1797)
Lovers' Vows (1798)
The Wise Man of the East (1799)
The Massacre (1792 (not performed)
A Case of Conscience (published 1833)
The Ancient Law (not performed)
The Hue and Cry (unpublished)
Young Men and Old Women (Lovers No Conjurers) (adaptation of Le Méchant; unpublished)

Novels

A Simple Story (1791)
Nature and Art (1796)

www.ingramcontent.com/pod-product-compliance
Lightning Source LLC
Chambersburg PA
CBHW021940040426
42448CB00008B/1167